Gray's Anatomy

Spalding Gray's monologues include
Sex and Death to the Age 14, Swimming to Cambodia,
The Terrors of Pleasure, and *Monster in a Box.*
His novel, *Impossible Vacation,* was published in 1992.
He lives in New York City.

Spalding Gray

Gray's Anatomy

PICADOR

First published 1994 by Vintage Books
a division of Random House, Inc., New York
and simultaneously in Canada by Random House of Canada Limited

First published in Great Britain 1994 by Picador
a division of Pan Macmillan Publishers Limited
Cavaye Place London SW10 9PG
and Basingstoke

Associated companies throughout the world

ISBN 0 330 33665 7
Copyright © Spalding Gray 1993

The development of the live performance of this work was in part made
possible by the Scottsdale Cultural Council. Portions of this work were
originally published in slightly different form in *The New York Times
Magazine* and *The San Francisco Chronicle*.

9 8 7 6 5 4 3 2 1

A CIP catalogue record for this book is available from
the British Library

Printed and bound in Great Britain by
Cox & Wyman Ltd, Reading, Berkshire

To Renée, with loving gratitude

Acknowledgments

I'd like to thank Linda Greenberg and Amanda Burroughs for their support in the development of this monologue. Also, Suzanne Gluck for her persistence in once again getting my voice in print. And finally, Renée Shafransky for her artistic collaboration on this project.

It happened that one of the twelve, Thomas, was absent when Jesus came. The other disciples kept telling him: "We have seen the Lord!" His answer was, "I will never believe it without probing the nailprints in his hands, without putting my finger in the nailmark and my hand into his side."

John 24:25

Gray's Anatomy

I think it all began when I was doing a storytelling workshop in upstate New York. I had about fifteen people I was working with. I asked them to sit in a circle as a kind of centering exercise before we began telling stories, and just look into each other's eyes. Not to speak but to just look into each other's eyes—and when they got tired of looking into one person's eyes they could move on to someone else's.

I was participating in this exercise, and I got locked into the eyes of this one particular woman. And I couldn't get out. Her name was Azaria Thornbird. She was tall, blonde, blue eyes, about thirty-six years old, dressed in white, the Immaculate Conception. I was riveted to her blue eyes. I couldn't take my eyes off her eyes. I couldn't move on to anyone else. And as I looked

3

into her eyes, her entire face began to slide off her skull. It was pouring down; it was drooling off like in a horror movie, like a bad LSD trip; and then her face turned into an oval ball of pulsing white light. I'd never seen anything like it, except on the cover of a Carlos Castaneda book. It was burning my retinas and dilating my pupils. I couldn't take my eyes off it. But all of a sudden the ball of white light came into a point and went Pfffff! Whoom! and vanished out the window behind her head, and her face recomposed and smiled back at me.

My rational, logical mind kicked right in and said, Uh, that was just a case of backlighting, wasn't it? She was sitting with the window behind her head. That was causing my pupils to dilate. It was backlighting. That was what that was, that was a case of extreme backlighting.

After the workshop, I went back home to work on my novel, *Impossible Vacation,* and I was reading a particularly painful section over and over. I found that as I was looking at the text the print on the manuscript page wasn't holding together. So I started fooling around and testing my eyes: I'd cover my left eye, and the print was fine looking through my right eye. I'd cover my right eye, and I saw that no matter where I held the text, I could never get it focused with my left eye, which kind of frightened me, because if it had to do with glasses, at some point I should be able to get it in focus.

But I didn't rush off to an optometrist, because I

wanted to finish my book first, and I thought I never would finish if I did that. I was a little frightened, really. I hadn't had my eyes examined in a long time, and I was fantasizing about all sorts of things—you know, CMV, retinitis, or a brain tumor. And I was secretly getting out Renée's Mayo Family Clinic disease book, which is this huge blue book the size of Webster's unabridged dictionary. She gave it to me for Christmas, but I can't look at the damn thing. The color photographs are unbelievable: of penis cancer, and galloping melanoma. . . . I couldn't even look at the section on eyes.

It was a good four months before I got the courage to go to an optometrist. I got a recommendation for a Dr. Schecter on the Upper East Side. So I went—I didn't tell him anything—and he begins the standard examination, by shining a light into my right eye, then over to my left, then back into my right, and over to my left again, and then starting with the right, and then back to the left very quickly. Then he starts concentrating on my left eye; left, left, left, left. He gets out another instrument and begins to peer into my left eye even more intensely. . . . It was like a scene from "General Hospital"; the only thing missing was the dramatic music.

He performs a very careful examination of my left eye, and finally he pulls back, puts all his instruments down, and says, "I think you have a problem with the retina of your left eye. But I can't tell you what it is, because I'm not an ophthalmologist. I'd like to recommend that you go to one. I can recommend one to you, and I think you should go to him *this afternoon*."

I rush out of there in a panic.

He recommends Dr. Mendel on the Upper West Side. So that means I have to run across the park from the Upper East Side to the Upper West Side, and I was running, believe me, I was running to get to Dr. Mendel's office. But I was also covering my right eye with my hand and looking through my left eye, thinking, My God, things are not good! I did not notice this much distortion before. The trees are all wavy; there are no straight lines in this park.

I get over to Dr. Mendel's office, and I go into Dr. Mendel's waiting room. The first thing they do is put drops in my eyes. I didn't know what they were for; I'd never had this done before. They did it to dilate my pupils, but they didn't tell me that. I was just sitting there trying to catch up on my reading, which I often do in doctors' offices. It's my one chance to catch up on *People*, *Newsweek*, and *Time*. What else is there to do in a doctor's office? I mean, you don't look at "the art."

So I'm sitting there reading and I did not know that they had dilated my pupils, and so gradually I'm going blind in the waiting room of that office. The whole place is turning into a fuzzball, just a big yellow fuzzball. It's horrible. There's nothing to do but sit there and wait. That's what I was doing; I was waiting in the waiting room.

6

I hated it. Finally, the nurse brought me into the doctor's office. Dr. Mendel introduced himself; he put me into the examination chair, got out a huge syringe, and told me that he was going to shoot me up with colored dye. Well, I thought, why not, he's the doctor.

I had to get him to explain everything to me. Why the dye? Well, it turns out that he wanted to take some photographs of my eye, and in order to photograph the vessels you have to have some dye in them.

He shoots me up. My vessels get filled with colored dye very quickly. He and the nurse tilt me forward and put my chin on a kind of brace. I'm looking through these two holes, into what I didn't know at the time was the camera, and they begin to take photos, and the camera turns out to be a flash camera, and these flashbulbs are going off right in my eyes. It's like a torture. I feel like I'm being blinded and I try to pull my head back but the nurse keeps pushing my head forward —*Flash flash flash!* It's like a *Clockwork Orange* situation. It's really like a torture. I come out reeling; all I can see is spots.

They finish, and the doctor rushes off, his gown blowing in the nonexistent breeze. He doesn't say a word. He's madly taking notes on a little pad as he goes off to develop the pictures. By now the nurse has stopped pushing my head and instead is holding my hand and talking about some vacation she wants to take in the Bahamas. And I am sitting there waiting. Dilated and waiting.

Finally the doctor comes back, but he does not come over to me. Instead he goes over to the telephone and calls Dr. Schecter, my optometrist, who's not in but has an answering machine. So Dr. Mendel begins dictating this message into Dr. Schecter's answering machine. He begins by saying, "Hello, Dr. Schecter, this is Dr. Mendel calling. First of all, I want to thank you for sending over your patient Gary Spalding."

Then he proceeds to dictate from his pad: "Close inspection of the left macula shows that there is a distortion of the interior limiting membrane secondary to the posterior hyloid face contraction. But the posterior hyloid, which was attached to the optic nerve macula, and major vessels of the retina, have remained attached and intact."

I say, "Dr. Mendel, over here please, could you please please tell me what is wrong with my left eye. Please . . . over here!"

He turns his back on me and continues dictating.

"With dissolution of the central vitreous gel, the envelope that the vitreous gel is in begins to shrink and distort the surface of the retina. A fluorozine angiogram has been done to the eye to determine the amount of vascular distortion. I was . . . surprised to see that he has some minimal cystoid macula edema in that left eye on the basis of the capillary incompetence from that distortion thank you!"

I said, "Dr. Mendel, what is wrong with my left eye? PLEASE!"

He said, "Basically, Gary, you have a macula pucker."

(Ahh—you laugh. All of my friends laughed when I told them that. They said, "Yeah, I knew a girl in high school named Macula Pucker, and she had syphilis.")

I said, "What is a macula pucker?"

"Basically, Gary, what's happened is the vitreous humor or the jelly in your eye has broken down, dissolved, liquefied, due to a trauma or age—we don't know what yet—and it's pulled away from the retina and left a little piece of skin or edema on the macula— the macula being the center of the retina, which is responsible for all detail in sight. Now this doesn't happen to everyone, but in your case what's happened is this. You have to imagine that your macula is kind of like a piece of Saran Wrap, and it's agitated and puckering up. It's puckering; it's a pucker. That's what it is; you have a pucker."

"Uhh . . . I see. I mean, how could this have happened? I don't want this to happen to my right eye! What what what could possibly be the cause?"

"Well, did you have any blows, any traumas to your left eye recently?"

"No, I don't think so. The last thing I can think of was in 1976—I was at a New Year's Eve party and I was dancing with a woman who did not have a very good sense of her own personal space, if you know what I mean? Her little pinky flew into my left eye and the fingernail of her pinky scratched my cornea. It was very

9

painful; it was running. I had a patch. You know, it was watering. It was awful."

He just looks at me and he says, "You have a good memory, don't you, Gary?"

So I said, "What are we going to do? How can this be helped?"

He said, "I recommend a little macula scraping."

Now as soon as I heard that word *scraping* I knew that I wanted a second, third, and fourth opinion.

He said, "Don't bother, really, I'm the best one around. I'm the only one who can do it."

Up until now, I did not really like this man. Now I really really did not like him, and I had to get out of that office. I went and told Renée what was going on, and she immediately wanted to find the best macula scraper in the United States.

Renée is great at that. When it comes to research on anything, she's great. I'm better at reflecting endlessly on what the causes might be. This is what I am obsessed with—not looking for another doctor. So, while Renée was looking for a doctor, I was keeping a journal analyzing what might have caused this strange eye condition.

First of all, I thought it might be the book—the book that I was writing, *Impossible Vacation*. It was simply too painful. It was about my mother's suicide, and I felt I really had never properly grieved for her, or mourned her, and what happened was, my eye—my left eye just cried, in a big way. It just exploded into one big tear from reading that painful section of the book over and over again. The entire vitreous humor just wept.

And then I began to think, no, it was because the book was written in the first person. It was too much, *I, I, I, I, I, I I I I I I I I I iiiiii!*

Then I thought it was my right brain rebelling against my left brain. Or my left brain rebelling against my right. Whenever I asked any New Age friends, particularly on the West Coast, what they thought caused it, they would say, "Well, what is it you *don't want to see . . . ?*"

I had lists! I was sure it had to do with my Oedipus complex, because my novel was essentially about that. And I was reading Freud's essay on negation at the time. Not that I'd ever been aware of wanting to sleep with my mother, but Freud says that the denial of some state of affairs is an implicit acknowledgment of it.

So if a guy says that he never wanted to sleep with his mother, he's as good as admitting that he at least gave it some solid consideration. So I'm thinking, the unconscious part of me, the part that did give it some consideration, is reaching up and scratching out one eye at a time, starting with the left eye, which is the feminine eye, in punishment for this . . . for not not sleeping with my mother.

Meanwhile, while I'm doing all this important speculation on the cause of this, Renée has found this wonderful Chinese doctor who she thinks is the right man. Highly recommended. I go meet him and I think, if anyone's going to do it, he's the guy. He's got a wonderful bedside manner. He's got a smile like Buddha. He's not like most eye doctors, who are automatons. He has great style, and, also, I like his use of language. He says, "What has to be done is a little macula peeling." And I like that a whole lot better than Dr. Mendel's "macula scraping."

He also says, "Don't worry about what the causes are, because your condition is idiopathic. Meaning, no known cause."

I also like him better than Dr. Mendel because he was not in a rush to operate; first he wants to tell me about the operation. "It's microsurgery," he says. "It's about ten years old, it costs ten thousand dollars, and there's no guarantee that it's going to work completely, but it might be helpful in bettering your sight. We'll cut into the white of your eye in two places in order to insert the peeler and a small pump. Then we'll put a microscope through the iris of the eye. Then we'll just go in and peel that pucker."

He wants to tell me what the risks of the operation are, of course. He tells me that there is a one to two percent chance of infection, which would mean prosthesis. One to two percent chance of a tear, which would mean being immediately blind in the left eye. There is a thirty-five percent chance of a cataract due to the trauma from the operation. And then there is a one percent chance of the whole condition just clearing up on its own.

Which I'm banking on.

But he's not in a rush to operate. He tells me that I have to check in with him every so often to see if the condition deteriorates any further, and if so then we should move on it. But right now we can let it ride and see if it does correct itself on its own.

I like this. I said, "Does that mean that I have time now, that I can do alternative therapies, you know, like diet, acupuncture, or prayer . . . or all three?"

"Oh yes, you can do alternatives," he says, with a sweet Buddha smile. "You can try them all. . . . And then we'll have to operate."

So I go back and I tell Renée what the doctor's told me, and she says, "Spald, do you know what *prosthesis* means?"

I said, "You know, I always thought I did, until this moment. It's one of those fuzzy words. It's nothing to do with the prostate gland. . . . Oh, doesn't it mean, like, false arm or false leg?"

And she said, "Try eye, Spald. Try glass eye."

Now I didn't want to go into the hospital, particularly after hearing this and going over the facts. A friend of mine went in not too long ago for a simple gallbladder operation, and the nurse gave him a shot in the wrong quadrant of his buttock, as they call it in the hospital, and it hit his sciatic nerve, paralyzed his right leg, and now he's suing the hospital for a million dollars. Renée went in for an operation a few years ago, and the day she went in, the *New York Post* had a cover story about some disgruntled hospital worker in that very hospital where Renée was, who had been fired and was so angry he had been putting horse tranquilizers in the IVs before he left.

Some years ago, I had a girlfriend in Boston who once had an affair with an OB/Gyn. She would go to the hospital to have the affair with him because he was always there delivering babies, and he had his own little cubicle with a bed to make love in. She also went there because he had access to liquid cocaine. She said they would rub liquid cocaine on all their body parts, and then they would smoke this really strong marijuana. They would begin to have sex, and, in the middle of all this, his beeper would go off. Off he would run, stoned, with an erection, to deliver a baby!

I didn't want to go into a hospital if I could help it.

Look, I grew up in Christian Science, so I didn't have a lot of experience with hospitals. I didn't have any connection with them, or doctors, for that matter. I mean, as Christian Scientists we were taught that disease, any kind of disease, was called error, that was it, error. I didn't know until I grew up that *error* meant an error in my thinking. Not in God's thinking but in mine, which I had to correct, you see. It's a very guilt-producing situation.

As a kid, I didn't know what the word *error* meant. Before I even knew that error meant mistake, I, as a little child, thought that error was a little green man, like little Peter Pain, who ran up on your arm in the night with a little pitchfork and went *stab, stab, stab* and gave you a sore throat. That was the way I perceived error as a child.

Now I can remember that once when I was a kid my cocker spaniel got hit by a car, not killed but wounded, and the cocker spaniel went, "Errorerror! Errorerrorerror! Errorerror! Errorerror!" And my mother said, "You see, Spuddie dear, even the dog knows."

It was kind of a lonely situation, being a Christian Scientist in Barrington, Rhode Island. There was no Christian Science church there. We'd go to church in Providence, and there were only five of us—my brothers and me, and two brothers from down the street. Occasionally my friends would do a ritual where they would get together, my Protestant and my Congregational friends, and occasional Catholics, and they would back me into a corner and do their own kind of Inquisition. They'd start in on me out of nowhere and say, "You are a Christian Scientist, right?"

"Yeah."

"You don't believe in doctors, huh?"

"That's right."

"Um. Say if lightning hit this branch here and it fell down and hit your head and knocked your brains out and your brains were spilling out all over the ground. Would you go to a doctor then?"

"No."

"Uh . . . Say you were walking across the street and a cement mixer came along and pulverized the whole lower part of your body. Would you go to a doctor thennnnnn?"

"No I wouldn't."

"Say the North Koreans invaded Barrington, Rhode Island, and they took a cage of hungry rats and put them up to your ass and they started eating up through your body. Would you go to a doctor thennnnn?"

"No."

I began to feel my friends had a death wish for me.

It put me on the outside of the community in a way. I did have some healings, though, but nothing super big. I mean, I can remember the first one that happened to me with a practitioner. I must have been twelve or thirteen years old, and I had this little stalactite, this little piece of flesh growing off the end of my nose. I don't know where it came from, or what it was. It looked horrible. It looked like snot, basically, and all my friends were saying, "Wipe your nose. You got snot on your nose!"

And I'd say, "It's not snot, it's not!"

It really was more embarrassing than pimples, and I wanted it cauterized. I was moving away from the faith. I said, "Please, Mom, I want to go to a doctor and have it burned off."

She said, "No, Spuddie dear. No, please, let's give it a week of prayer and see what happens."

It was another embarrassing week before she called a Christian Science practitioner, and everyone was praying: he was praying, I was praying, my mother was praying for the little stalactite to drop off. By the end of the week it hadn't dropped off, so I wanted to go to the doctor on Monday but Mom said, "Please, Spuddie dear, give it one more day."

On that particular Monday I was being tutored. I was failing seventh-grade math, and I was being tutored by this lovely older woman who just kept looking at my nose until she finally said, "Looks like you need a hankie!"

So I was trying to humor her. She brought over a linen hankie; I just took her handkerchief and lightly wiped my nose.

And it came off!

Keeping this healing in mind, remembering this event, I decided my first alternative choice would be to call a Christian Science practitioner, which I'd never done in my adult life. Really, my mother had always done it for me.

She was dead; she couldn't do it now.

So I did it. I called. I called from London, actually, to San Francisco. Of course the power of prayer is supposed to go around the world, so I didn't think there was any problem with the distance. I got him on the phone. Look, when you're dealing with a Christian Science practitioner and you're talking about the disease, you really have to be quite careful not to name it. You're not supposed to name it, because to name it gives it power. You're supposed to refer to it as "an error."

That word *error* has a lot of innuendo when the practitioner uses it to find out what's wrong. You know, like, Is it a big error? Like cancer or AIDS? Or is it a little error, like a cold? Or a minor error, like the flu?

Well, I start right in and say, "It's my left eye, actually."

And he says, "I know quite enough, thank you. Don't say any more. I think I can begin praying, and I'm going to send you some information about eyes from Mary Baker Eddy's *Science and Health*. Then let's get *on* this together and try to clear this up. But I want to ask you something first, Spalding, before I take you on. . . . Are you faithful?"

I said, "Um, do you mean am I full of faith?"

"No, are you seeing anyone else. Any doctors."

"Well, um, there's this Chinese doctor in my life actually. . . . It's not very serious. I haven't seen him in a while. I have to check in with him every so often. But we're not going steady or anything like that."

"Well, I'm afraid we can't do that; we can't be duplicitous in our faith. You have to make up your mind whether to go with a Christian Science practitioner or a doctor, but you can't divide your faith that way."

"Really? Well, gosh, *he* said I could see other people!"

"Well, I can't work that way, and I'm afraid you're going to have to think about it and call me up when you make up your mind."

I hung up, realizing why it was I had left Christian Science in the first place.

I went to my therapist to talk to him about it. My

therapist was a graduate of Auschwitz; he was an existential realist. And I went in to talk to him about my condition, and he said, "Spalding, Spalding, please. All things are contingent, and there is also chaos. . . . In other words . . . shit happens. Give up on this magical thinking and this airy-fairy Disneyland kind of let's pretend and your Hollywood la-la fantasy, please. Do the right thing. Get the operation. Hmmn?"

He was no help.

I left his office, really down, depressed, wandering, walking the way I do when I get upset in New York. I just walk the city. I was walking, walking, and I was real shabby looking; I hadn't shaved. I was dressing like I felt—really down and out—and my coat was all frayed. I was thinking, How can I do this? I can't go into the hospital and have someone cut into my eye. How can I let someone cut into my eye with a knife, with a scalpel, cut into the window of my soul? And also, what is this thing with the detail? Why of all things should I be losing my ability to see detail? This is what I totally depend on in order to tell stories. I tell stories about the details of things. If I lost the detail in my right eye, what could I possibly do? There is no way I could make a living. What am I going to be, a blind poet in New York City? I don't even know how to write poetry! I don't even *like* poetry!

I'm thinking about this as I'm walking with my head down, all over the city, and I find myself down in the Bowery, which is now a perfect place for me to be. I feel right at home there, the way I'm dressed and the way I'm looking and feeling. I'm wandering through this gaggle of prostitutes who are working out of the johns' cars; they just get in the cars and ride around the block —and I'm walking past them, and I'm noticing out of the corner of my good eye that there's this black Pontiac pulling up, and they're all rushing to it like flies.

They're over there all bunched around the Pontiac and I'm walking by, and one of them turns and yells, "Yo! Hey, boy! They want you!"

I turn, because I'm curious, and I love to be wanted.

I move closer, and the prostitutes part, like the Red Sea. I walk right through, and see this old black Pontiac with three Hasidic Jews in it, two in the front and one in the back.

And they say, "Get in."

And . . . I do. Because I'm curious.

Look, I figured I was safe. I didn't think anyone could impersonate a Hasidic Jew. I mean, if there were three priests in the car, I would not have gotten in.

I sat in the back seat with the youngest one, and there was no sexual vibe in the car at all. I didn't know what they wanted, but there was no sexual vibe. We drive off, and the prostitutes are yelling, "Good-bye! Have a good trick, babe! Have a good trick!"

We're riding in the car and my new companions say, "Do you want any beer or pizza?"

I say, "No, I never drink before five, and I've already eaten. So what's up?" By now I'm calling myself Peter and saying I'm a drifter from Schenectady. I've taken on this new identity. I wanted a vacation from Spalding Gray; I'm just sick of myself and my bad eye. I'm trying to be Peter with perfect eyes, that's what I'm pretending.

I say, "Where are we going?"

And they say, "We're taking you to Williamsburg to clean our synagogue."

I think, Oh my God, well, why not? You know, it's a nice vacation; it's a nice way to tour New York. I've never been to Williamsburg; I don't believe we're going to do this.

But we did it. We drove over the Williamsburg Bridge, then pulled up in front of this small synagogue. I go in and all these Hasidim are there, with twinkling eyes, looking up at me like little Santa Clauses. They're repairing the bindings on old books. They take me to the back door, and, listen, I know that at any point I can say, "I'm Spalding Gray," and just walk out. But I'm not doing that. I'm taking it in: They give me a dustpan and a rake and a broom and a shovel, and they say, "Clean. Please, clean our backyard."

I go into the backyard and I start raking. I'm feeling great. I'm raking up the leaves, I am sweeping up the broken white plastic knives and forks, and paper cups and plates left over from parties, and I'm whipping it up! I'm doing such a great, energized job that this woman who lives in the building behind the synagogue throws up her windows and cries out, "Hey boy! You work good! You come here next?"

I say, "I'm all booked up. Sorry. This is it for the day."

In an hour's time I have that whole backyard just perfect. I have everything in piles, get everything into trash bags. The Hasid who was driving the car comes down and says, "You work good. You are the best, hardest-working Bowery bum we have ever picked up." It turns out that every Sunday they go and pick up Bowery bums and bring them over to clean the place.

He says, "Usually we just give them drinks, but you don't drink, so we have to pay you. How much, huh? Eight. I think eight dollars."

I say, "No, no, ten. . . . It's ten dollars an hour."

"Eight plus carfare."

"No, ten and I'll walk."

"No. Eight."

Here we are, a Scot and a Jew, haggling over money in the back of a synagogue.

I get the ten dollars and I walk. I'm walking over the Brooklyn Bridge back to the city feeling triumphant! I think, there *is* something I can do if I lose my sight in my right eye. I can do something other than tell stories!

Shortly after this event we have a reunion of the storytelling workshop that I did upstate. A number of people show up. I'm very excited that Azaria Thornbird is one of them, because I didn't think she'd come. She lives in the Minneapolis area, and I didn't think she'd fly from that far away. I was excited that she came, because she was one of the most interesting people in that workshop. And not just because her head turned into a ball of light.

How to describe her? It's difficult, really. She's a single mother, a very good mother I think, of two pretty normal sons. She raised them on her own. But also she's trained with this very controversial and perverse American Indian sorceror. He's named Everet K. Whiteowl, and he works with a group outside of Salt Lake City in the deserts. He's half German and half Native-American Indian. He also trained as a marine, so he has this theory—at least, this is what I was told; I'm just repeating what I heard—that in order to learn how to heal, you must first learn how to kill. So he and his disciples perform all these rituals where they shoot each other with paint bullets and bury each other alive with just a blanket over the top of the grave for forty-eight hours, no food or water; they dance back and forth at a tree for two days, back and forth with no food or water. They do tantric training; they do martial arts.

This is quite an initiation that Azaria has gone through, but she's no longer going out to see him. She could no longer afford that. Instead, she's gotten to a place . . . well, here's the part that is difficult to describe, because I'm not sure what exactly is happening here. What she says happens is that she goes to bed, and she has an astral body that comes out of her corporal body at night and gets up and walks around the house looking for various Indian grandmothers and then meets Everet's astral body. Their astral bodies get together to talk in order to save money on airfare. They meet in what they call a lucid dream state or a kind of waking dream. Then she goes back into her body; and Everet Whiteowl's astral body flies back to California.

I said, "My God, you mean a part of you can get up and look back at your body?"

She said, "Yes."

I said, "Didn't you ever consider making love to yourself?" Because, I mean, that's the first thing I would want to do if I found myself leaving my body.

"No," she said; no, she hadn't. Another time when I met her after this she said that she had tried it and that it had worked.

When she tells me these stories, I absolutely believe them, because there's something so completely believable in her tone of voice. In fact she showed me where Everet had grabbed her arm and left black-and-blue marks. She said she wasn't going to work with him much longer, because of the aggressive way in which his astral body grabbed her astral body.

The other thing she learned from him was called Breath of Fire. She showed it to me and I'd never seen anything like it in my life. She lay on the floor and had about six orgasms in a row. It was like a Reichian dream. She came six times without ever touching herself. She just lay there—her whole body quivering

24

and shaking as she came six times from her toes to her nose.

I said, "Teach me! Teach me!! TEACH ME!!! Do you know how many lonely nights I spend in motels and hotels? I would give anything to be able to come like that without touching myself!"

So she tried. She had me lie down, and she said I had to breathe in through my coccyx. I didn't quite know what that was. She said I should take the energy in through the base of my spine and up. . . . I tried, but the closest I could get to it was sort of a feeling of reverse farting. I couldn't get it.

Anyway, needless to say, this is one very powerful and interesting lady, and she showed up at our storytelling reunion. We started talking about my eye and she said, "You must come out to do an Indian sweat with my group." She had an Indian lodge out there, outside of Minneapolis.

I said, sure, I would do that.

She said, "You have to realize that, when you get with a group, praying, the power of feeling is much greater in a group situation than it is one-on-one. So you must do it. You must promise me."

I said yes, I would: the way I always do to—to everything.

Well, I didn't go to this one. I don't know why. But she was insistent. She kept calling and leaving messages on our answering machine. Renée would often end up taking them off the machine, and she began to get very aggravated and say, "What are you getting involved with now? Some sort of sweat cult?"

I went out, and it was winter in Minneapolis. A group of us—I think there were probably seventeen of us, men and women—did this incredible ceremony that Azaria led with a peace pipe, where she called all the Indian spirits from the four directions. We were all in a barn. We followed her out through knee-deep snow to the sweat lodge. If you haven't seen an Indian sweat lodge, it's a dome about five feet high and it's made of bent branches and saplings tied together. The Indians, I guess, covered theirs with buffalo robes and animal skins. I think this one had a canvas and plastic tarp over it. Rocks had been heating up all morning in a big pit to be brought into the lodge, and there was cold water to be poured on top of them.

Azaria led us all out through the knee-deep snow to the sweat lodge, then she said, "Take off your clothes and throw them in the snow."

We do. I'm doing everything I am told here. It's damned cold, and I'm like a shivering refugee. There are seventeen naked men and women all shivering in the snow. We line up outside the sweat tent and I'm trying to get to the front of the line, to get into the tent as soon as I can. I end up fourth in line. And I'm just standing there, freezing, looking around, and I realize that there are really no American Indians there.

Basically, these people are Scandinavian. They all have blond hair and blue eyes.

So, we're standing outside the tent, and Azaria tells us to cry out to the sky, as we enter, "All my ancestors!" Just cry it out to the sky.

Each person begins, "All my ancestors! All my ancestors!" They cry to the sky as they enter the tent.

My turn comes, and I yell, "All my ancestors!" And then I think, Wait a minute. All my ancestors? My father just finished the family tree. It took him six years to do it. I'd been looking it over, so I had a good sense of who they were. I remembered John Proctor, and the Right Reverend Curtis Fox Gray and his wife Thankful Atherton Gray, Colonel Simeon Spalding, Captain Edward Spalding, Brigadier General John Crane, the only man wounded in the Boston Tea Party. And I thought, All my ancestors—who were they? Pilgrims. What did they do shortly after they came to America? Kill the Indians. Where was I going? Into an Indian sweat lodge!

GOOOOOOOD LUCK!!!!!!!!!!

At last we are all inside the tent and we sit naked in a circle on straw which is laid over the snow. It's dark and it's cold in there because no hot rocks have been brought in yet. Azaria instructs us that there are going to be four rounds of prayers. In the first round we'd be praying for some conscious intention, some attitude or state of mind that we wished to maintain during the sweat ceremony, which could last quite a long time, two or three hours. In the second round, we'd be praying for friends, others, loved ones who are needy. And in the third, we'd give away some thing, some condition that we no longer wanted. Say, like an eye condition? But, she warns us, in no case—in *no case*—should we identify with what another person gives away. Because if we take it on, we're going to be in trouble. So just pass it on; don't identify with it, just pass it on, and let it go out of the tent. And round number four is that she will come and pour cold water over the rocks, and we're supposed to sit in silence and listen to the hot rocks steam—and they often actually speak and give us valuable information. That's what Azaria told us.

I like this very much, this whole very ritualized ceremony. You're supposed to start out the prayer by saying, "O Great Spirit, my name is . . . ," and then you give your name, and you do the prayer, and then, in order to indicate that you've finished, you say, "I have spoken."

I like this. I just hope that people don't go on. I mean, there are seventeen people in there, after all, and I hope the prayers aren't too long, because it's going to get real hot.

So we begin, and the fire-keeper brings in the first hot rocks, and they're put into a pit. Azaria pours some water over them and they sizzle, but it's still quite cold in there. The first prayer begins, with prayer for some state of mind or condition that we'd like to maintain in the ceremony. People begin praying:

"O Great Spirit. This is Shelly speaking, and I want to maintain an alert, present state of mind here. I have spoken."

"O Great Spirit, this is Robert speaking, and I want to remain humble. If anything else, most of all, I want to be humble and get rid of all my macho qualities for this ceremony. I have spoken."

It comes around to me, and I say, "O Great Spirit, this is Spalding speaking, and I pray that I can maintain a sincere and open attitude in this ceremony and not pollute it with my heady analysis and ironic commentary and end up turning this sacred event into just another story that I will try to sell to the American public."

And the entire tent goes, "Ho! Ho! Ho! Ho! Ho!" Which is a kind of supportive cheer to say, let's see if you can pull that one off.

More hot rocks are brought in. Azaria pours cold water on them and Pzzzchhh! now it's starting to get a little hot. Oh man, I know what they mean by sweat! And my God, I've got my nose down on the ground trying to breathe fresh air from under the bottom of the tent. And all I can see is the sign on the outside of the steam bath at my health club in New York City that says DO NOT EXCEED FIFTEEN MINUTES UNDER ANY CIRCUMSTANCES! And I'm thinking, Who is this Azaria Thornbird, anyway?!

You know, so her head turned into a ball of white light—is that supposed to protect me? How long have I been in here? What's going on?

And we pray for friends. I pray for Renée. I pray that Renée will be able to get a good job in Hollywood writing a film script that is both interesting and entertaining, funny, and that will *get made*. Before that place burns down or falls into the sea. I also pray for my friends with AIDS.

More hot rocks are brought in, lots. Now the place is really hot; the place is reeking. People are down on their sides, choking; they can't breathe. My pulse is up to 160. Now the third round starts; we're supposed to give something away. I can't wait to pray. I'm telling you I feel like my heart is going to explode. I've got my hand on my pulse, it's so hot I can't breathe, and people are praying:

"O Great Spirit, I want to give away my pride. I have spoken."

"O Great Spirit, I want to give away my greed. I have spoken."

"O Great Spirit, this is Ron speaking. I want to give away my jealousy. I have spoken."

"This is Susan speaking. O Great Spirit, I want to give away my gluttony. I have spoken."

It comes round to me and I say, "O Great Spirit, this is Spalding speaking. And I want to give away the fear that I'm about to have a heart attack at this very moment!"

And just as I say this the guy next to me, who is about my age, leaps up and runs out of the tent, screaming, "My heart is popping! My heart is popping! My heart is popping!"

And I'm FINE!

My pulse slows down. He's just taken all my fear and run right out the door with it.

Azaria says, "Someone has broken the sacred circle here. The power has gone out of the sweat. Now listen, we're going to do the fourth round of prayers, where we'll listen to the hot rocks talk. If any of you feels you have to go, you must leave now. Because when this flap shuts . . . you're in."

Oh my. Now I at the same time am very claustrophobic and find it difficult to take orders. But I am determined to ride this thing out. I sit hard and I just hope that the hot rocks don't talk too long, you know?

She says, "I'm closing the flaps." She closes it, and this guy who's a member of the lodge, with a ponytail down to his ass, leaps up and charges for the flap. She throws her naked body in front of him and says, "Get back, Lame Deer! GET BACK!"

He hurls himself back on the hay crying, "Shit, fuck fuck fuck. . . ." Everyone's holding him down, chanting, "Ho! Ho! Ho! Ho! Ho!" Everyone's Ho-ing him, Ho-ing him, Ho-ing him until at last he's calm.

We sit there panting, and we listen to the hot rocks talk. I didn't understand a word.

31

But I walked out of the tent feeling good, triumphant. I mean, I felt good that I had made it through this ordeal, and my body felt good. I don't know how long it had been in there; maybe two and a half hours. I'd lost all sense of time. The sun was setting, casting a red glow over the snow. It was just spectacular. I could roll in the snow, I felt such internal body heat radiating from me. I felt really triumphant!

But Azaria takes me aside and says, "What's wrong?"

"Nothing. I feel great for the first time in my life!"

"But Spalding, when the time came for you to give away your eye condition, you started babbling about a heart attack!"

"Oh my God. Oh no. Oh shit."

And I realized that I was still the child who acts on his most immediate fears.

I get back to New York City and go to Weiser's bookstore to look for books on healing. Why not heal yourself? God, why look for it somewhere else? I see a book on self-healing, and I think, now this is up my alley. It's written by a guy named Sebastian Sherborne, who lives out in Oakland. It's mainly about how he healed himself of cataracts with a very simple method, similar to the Bates method, which involves rubbing your hands together, then palming your eyes. It's called palming. So I go out to Oakland to work with him. He's quite expensive. He wants me to continuously rub my palms together. He tells me to get my palms very warm, to rub them about three to four hundred times and then to quickly cover my eyes with them for three to four hours. And it is unbearable. It is unbearable being stuck in all that darkness. I cannot tell you how dark it is, but that's what he wants: he wants me to see only darkness; he even has meditation tapes that start out with his slow, droning voice saying, "Cover your eyes and see all as black: your room as black; Oakland as black; all of California and the United States as black. Please see Europe and Africa as black." And on and on. This black incantation drones on for hours.

He told me, "No matter what you do, don't get an operation. It screwed up my eyes completely. Just keep rubbing your hands and palming."

I'm riding around San Francisco rubbing my hands and covering my eyes, causing incredible problems. I'm in a bus doing it, and a little girl behind me says, "Daddy, is the bus going to crash?" I go to a Shirley MacLaine concert in San Francisco with a friend, and I'm rubbing my hands and covering my eyes, and my friend asks, "Do you really think she's that bad?" Wherever I go, people come up beside me and ask, "Are you all right? Is there anything I can do for you?" Because I have my hands over my eyes they think I'm in despair. I'm getting a lot of attention, but my eyes aren't getting any better. I think, How is this going to help a macula pucker? Maybe it will help something else. The thing is, I can't stop doing it.

It's become this new compulsion for me. Wherever I go, I'm rubbing by hands together. I also realize that the more I look inside, the more I don't see a self to heal. I can't get any sense of such a thing. There's no core, no me. All I see is darkness, which is more and more frightening for me. It feels just like death. So I'm starting to give up on working with this healer, but I still can't stop rubbing my hands.

But in the end it was not the obsessive hand rubbing and the endless darkness that turned me off. It was the man himself. I gradually came to realize that Sebastian Sherborne was an egocentric, self-absorbed man. He was really too much like myself for me to be open to him. It all began when he first started to massage my eyes. Every time he did this he insisted on playing tapes of his radio interviews in the background, and, instead of pointing out sections about healing, he would call my attention to all the jokes he was making. It was as though he was a frustrated stand-up comedian who was stuck in the healing profession.

What really put me off was when we were doing an eye exercise in his backyard. Every day, he would sit me in a chair and ask me to close my eyes, tilt my face toward the sun and roll my head back and forth. After doing that for five minutes, I was to put my hands over my eyes and palm for ten minutes. Then I was to take my hands off my eyes and try to read an eye chart that he had tacked up on the wall. I have to admit that there were times that the letters on the chart seemed clearer and I could read more of the smaller lines. After a while I got sick of the eye chart, so I asked Sebastian if he had a picture or a photo he could hang up on the wall instead of the eye chart. He didn't say anything. He just went into the house and came out with a giant portrait of himself that one of his patients had painted and put it in front of me.

After I finished with Sebastian I went to visit friends in Berkeley. I was walking down Telegraph Avenue, and I stopped at my favorite little juice bar. The juice boy was very friendly with me, and I told him about my eye condition while I was palming in front of him. He gets all excited and says, "I know just the guy who can heal you. He's an authentic Brazilian healer, and he does healings every Friday."

So I think I'll give it a try, since I'm already in Berkeley. Why not? I've never been to an authentic Brazilian healer before. I go over on a Friday at eight o'clock and discover some sort of "healing society." The people are dressed in white and they're walking in circles, doing this defusing process in which they spin their hands very fast all around your body without touching you. In fact, they do it to you when you come into the house. I don't know if they're trying to create a new aura, or if they're trying to make it safe in the house by taking our street aura away. They give no explanation for it. The place is filled with some people dressed in white and some people dressed in regular street clothes, like me. There's one seat left, and I go in and sit down. Just as my backside touches the metal chair, the entire house rumbles, shakes, and levitates, and all the lights go off. The first thing I think is that I've caused it by sitting down. The second thing I think is that they're performing some sort of black magic. At last I realize that there's been an earthquake, because everyone's yelling, "Earthquake! Earthquake!" and they're all standing up from their chairs. I'm saying, "Earthquake? I thought I caused it!"

The woman next to me says, "You must be either very self-centered or very paranoid."

And I say, "Try both."

So they're in a panic, and this woman in the back—I liked her very much, your typical Berkeleyite, who was dressed in ripped, faded jeans and hiking boots—who was also there for the first time, yells, "That was an earthquake!"

The leader of the group tells everyone, "Breathe in deeply and bring the house down. Breathe in deeply and calm the earth, please."

But the woman yells again, "I want to know if this house is earthquake-proof!"

"Please," the leader says, "we will bring the house down by breathing. No panic, please."

So she yells, "Denial! Denial!"

Then she jumps up, goes out, slams the door, and all the lights come back on. They don't get a chance to defuse her before she reenters the real world.

After everyone calms down, I am finally taken back

to meet the leader. He looks like a combination of Dustin Hoffman and John Belushi. A very jolly kind of guy. He looks me right in the eye. I tell him I have a problem with my left eye, and he says, "I'm sorry to tell you, my friend, but someone worked black magic on you three years ago."

"Oh God, no," I say. "Black magic?" And I instantly know all the people who worked it on me as soon as he says that. I start making lists. "What's to be done?"

"We build a plaster of Paris canal and blow cigar smoke on it. We do this every Friday for two months."

So I say, "Uh, I'm really supposed to go dancing. I'm supposed to go dancing over in, uh, San Francisco."

I leave, call my doctor back in New York, and ask him how much time I have left. I tell him I've been sweating, I've been palming, I've had some black magic done on me, and I don't know where to turn next.

He says, "I think your time is running short. Really."

I get back to New York City, and I'm pretty depressed. I'm sitting there at the kitchen table with Renée, and I can't stop thinking about Azaria Thornbird and how she threw her naked body in front of Lame Deer to stop him from getting out of the tent. I'm thinking about it, and I'm also telling Renée about it —over and over again. Renée is sitting there at the table, and her leg's beginning to pump. She says, "Spald? If you're going to start hanging around with women who can teach you how to come without touching yourself, and hurl their naked bodies in front of men who are trying to save themselves from being steamed to death, I think we should get married. We've been together for twelve years now. Don't you think we should give it a try?"

"Married? I don't know. . . . I never . . . I just don't want to get married."

"But why?

"Um. I don't know. I don't have a reason. I just don't."

"No reason?"

"Well, I just get fuzzy when I think about it. It's not . . . I mean, I like being boyfriend and girlfriend. It makes me feel younger. But, I mean, husband and wife. It sounds so serious. It sounds so biblical, so Old Testament."

"But you're fifty years old. You don't want to be an old boy. I don't want to be an old girl. I mean, what is it that you're afraid of? What is the first thing you think of when I ask you about marriage?"

"Divorce. But it's not really just divorce, it's—"

"Spald. Grow up. Really."

"Well it's not. The ceremony, for instance. 'Till death do us part.' I don't want to be in a ceremony where they talk about death. Or 'for as long as they two shall live.' It's so depress—actually . . . it's my eye, come to think of it. Till I get this eye thing cleared up, I would rather not, you know. . . . I can't do both. I can't chew gum and walk at the same time. It's like a big thing to get married. And the eye is a big thing. So you see what I mean? It's kind of a crisis now. I promise, as soon as the eye is dealt with, I will discuss it in an adult way. You see, we have something to look forward to."

But also, I wanted Renée to stop talking because I wanted to hear the Barry Spires show that was on the radio in the background. It was noon, and I listen every noon. Barry Spires is the most radical nutritionist in the world. He probably sleeps about two hours a night and lives on air. When he can find it. I mean, I go and buy my health food at Whole Foods on Prince Street, to eat it while I listen to him, but I can't even eat. I'm trying to eat healthy, organic food, and I can't even eat that when I listen to him.

Because according to Barry, *everything* gives you cancer. And everything else heals you of it. So I'm listening, and at the end of the show, Renée, as usual, has a brilliant idea. She says, "Call him. Call Barry. Get a recommendation. See if he knows anyone who can help you."

So I do call. He's open; he's accessible after the show, when he's answering phone calls. And he's very sympathetic; he knows what a macula pucker is, and he says to me, "Have you ever heard of Dr. Ron A. Axe in Poughkeepsie?"

"Nope."

"Well, you should have, because he is the best nutritional ophthalmologist in the United States."

I get the telephone number and I call Dr. Ron A. Axe. This wizened old voice answers the phone. This old, ancient androgynous voice, it's like Tiresias, I don't know if it's male or female or what. I wondered how any doctor could allow a voice like this to answer the phone for him.

It's screaming and cackling, "HELLO?! HELLO? DR. AXE IS VERY BUSY! YOU CAN TAKE YOUR CHANCES IF YOU WANT TO COME OUT, BUT YOU'D BETTER COME EARLY BECAUSE OF THE EXTENSIVE DIETARY QUESTIONNAIRE! NOW IF YOU'RE TAKING THE TRAIN—"

I said, "I am."

"IF YOU'RE TAKING AMTRAK, TAKE IT FROM PENN STATION. GET OFF IN POUGHKEEPSIE AND WALK LEFT ON FAY STREET FOR THREE BLOCKS. YOU CAN'T MISS US!"

That's it. No address, no nothing. But it seemed like an important journey, and I thought that I probably should do what the old voice said.

I take the train up there, and I'm walking left down Fay Street. It's nothing but a desert out there. My God, it's tract houses. There's no landscaping, no trees. High tension wires.

I'm strolling along, I round the corner, and all of a sudden I see it. Bam! You can't miss it. It's like Fruit Loops! This house is like Hansel and Gretel's house on

40

acid. Like Howard Finster's dream. The shingles are the colors of the rainbow. There are Day-Glo frames around the windows. The stones that the house is on top of— the foundation—are red, yellow, blue, purple, and there is this little grove of pine trees, and a sign on one of the trees reads: DR. RON A. AXE, O.D. F.F.A.O. F.C.O.U.D. F.I.C.A. F.A.S.S. Out of the pine trees comes this spindly little elfin man, who must weigh only about 97 pounds, with these bottle-thick glasses on. And I'm thinking, I hope that's not Dr. Ron A. Axe.

It's not. It's Don B. Axe, his brother. And assistant. Don takes me into the sun porch to help me fill out the Dietary Questionnaire. I walk into the sun porch and I am overwhelmed by the business of the place. Quadraphonic opera is playing. *Madama Butterfly* full blast. There are ski medals all over the walls. There are miniature dinosaurs in a prehistoric landscape playing over in the corner. There's a six-foot cutout of Hoagy Carmichael standing in the corner. There's the toothless head of a Bengal tiger, roaring at me over in that corner. There's a four-foot-wide map of the moon framed in a pink Hula-Hoop on the ceiling. And streaming down the wall, like a paper waterfall, is the yellowing teletype printout of Lyndon Johnson's 1964 acceptance speech for the Democratic presidential nomination.

I'm looking. I'm looking everywhere like a little baby trying to take it all in.

And Don Axe is saying, "All this stuff makes you

41

want to see, doesn't it? Activates the eyes, gets them moving, doesn't it? Makes you want to look around; makes you really want to look!"

At last we get to the Dietary Questionnaire. Now listen to this. There are 742 questions on this, concerning everything I've eaten in the past six months. The categories are soups, meat, poultry, eggs, fish, seafood, dairy products, vegetables, desserts, sweets, beverages, grains, breads, cereals, nuts, seeds, legumes, fruits, spices, herbs, flavorings, condiments . . . miscellaneous items. And he begins with Burrito.

"All right. How many burritos have you had in the last six months?"

Now I have a fairly cinematic memory, and the visions of all those Mexican restaurants are flying at me. But I can't picture what was on the plate. Was it an enchilada, a taco?

I say, "The burritos are those little white football-shaped kind of things, aren't they?"

"Right, how many?"

I said, "Oh, oh . . . let's say—eighteen!"

"Eighteen burritos, eighteen. Were they whole wheat, or flour?"

I said, "What do you mean, whole wheat? Where do you get a whole wheat burrito? I don't travel in those circles."

"All right. Borscht. On to borscht. On to borscht. What about borscht?"

I said, "Borscht? I never encounter it. I never eat it or

drink it, or whatever it is you're supposed to do with it. I just don't run into borscht."

"All right. By—"

"But wait a minute, wait a minute. But if you say six months. . . . Come to think of it, just six months ago I was in Russia. And I had it every day. But I don't normally have it, so does that count?"

"Yes, it does. Of course it counts. Okay, six months ago. Well, how many days were you there?"

"I think fourteen."

"Fourteen. Fourteen. Well, we'll put down sixteen borschts, just to be safe. All right—hot dogs, hot dogs!"

I said, "I don't touch hot dogs. Just skip them—but come to think of it now, I was in Columbus, Ohio, a few months ago, and every day I went to this place called Coney Island—Well, actually, they called those wieners, so we'll wait till we get to *W,* all right?"

In the middle of this interrogation, the old voice from the telephone comes in. It happens to be his eighty-seven-year-old mother. She's got this babushka on, and these bottle-thick glasses. And she's yelling, "TIME TO BRING MR. GRAY INTO THE EXAMINATION ROOM. TIME FOR MR. GRAY TO GET INTO THE ELECTRIC CHAIR. TIME FOR MR. GRAY TO SEE DR. AXE."

"Mother, please. We have not finished the Dietary Questionnaire."

"BRING HIM IN. BRING HIM IN. BRING HIM ON INTO THE ANTECHAMBER!"

We go into this antechamber before we go in to see the doctor, and Ron follows, continuing the questionnaire.

"Rabbit, rabbit rabbit, how many rabbits?"

"Renée won't let it into the house."

"Snow rabbit, wild rabbit—?"

I said, "Just a minute." I am staring into the antechamber. I am overwhelmed by what I see in there. On the wall are two six-foot-high black-and-white cutouts of Toscanini and Caruso looking down at me. Underneath are cross-sabered miniature Walküries. There's opera playing. There's a map of the universe on the ceiling with Christmas balls hanging down from it at various levels. And I'm just a little overloaded by it all, and Don is babbling, "Rabbit, rabbit, dark meat or light, with skin or without it, do you cook it with or without it? Snow rabbit, or—"

"No rabbit, no rabbit—Please stop. Renée won't let it in the house."

"BRING HIM IN TO THE EXAMINATION CHAIR!!!"

I walk into Dr. Axe's office, and there is this spindly little elfin guy with bottle-thick glasses sitting behind a desk with a sign saying, DR. RON A. AXE, O.D. F.F.A.O. F.C.O.U.D. F.I.C.A. F.A.S.S.

He says, "Welcome, Mr. Gray. Please come in. Would you get in the electric chair."

So I get in this blue examination chair, which he refers to as the electric chair. I'm sitting there, and he begins to project on a screen across the room what I can only describe as a family slide show. I'm not questioning it. It's a picture of him and his brother skiing down Tuckerman's Ravine on Mt. Washington. It's a picture of him and his brother and his eighty-seven-year-old mother skiing in Stowe, Vermont. It's a picture of him and his brother and his eighty-seven-year-old mother at Lenin's tomb. And I'm saying, "Oh, I was just there myself, just six months ago, you know. That's where I had the fourteen borschts."

I'm chiming right in.

But in the middle of this—and I don't know how he does it technically—but it comes up in the slide, in the left-hand corner: an eye chart. But it's still *in* the slide; you see him and his family skiing behind the eye chart.

And he says, "Can you read that?"

And I can. Better than I can read it in my Chinese doctor's office. I don't know if I'm more relaxed, but I'm able to read more lines. I'm beginning to think, Wait, there's method in this man's *meshugaas*. I'm going to let him examine my eyes. At least I'll let him do that.

He begins. He looks at my retinas, and he sees the pucker in the left eye, and he begins to speculate. He says he's not sure yet, but he has a theory: "I don't know what caused this. But I'm going to speculate. Vitamin C. Do you take a lot of it?"

"Well, yes, I do. I have to in my profession, because I simply cannot afford to get a cold or sore throat. So I gobble it like crazy."

"Well, do you know what Vitamin C is?"

I said, "Well, um . . . I think it's Vitamin C."

"Wrong. It's ascorbic acid. And certain parts of the body can't pass it on. The vitreous humor and the pancreas, they hold on to Vitamin C. So what would you be doing, pouring acid into your eye, hmmm?

"Now if it isn't the ascorbic acid that's rotting out your vitreous humor, it's certainly the ozone layer. Because it's breaking down. You know the sheep are going blind in New Zealand. I hope you have a nice wide-brimmed hat and good sunglasses that have been treated for the ultraviolet rays. Do you?"

"No. I don't have a really good hat. I have a double crown, and I can't ever find a hat to fit me."

"I want you to have a complete blood test. I'm going to give you the chart here, and you have to take this in to a laboratory and have your blood drawn. We're going to find out every toxin that's in your body. Now pay my mother two hundred forty dollars for today."

So I go in and I pay the mother. Two hundred forty dollars. Uninsured. No insurance company will cover this. The mother is sitting there saying, "WHAT AM I GOING TO DO? MY SON DOES RESEARCH, RESEARCH, RESEARCH. WE DON'T HAVE ANY FUN ANYMORE. WE DON'T SKI. WE USED TO SKI. I'M EIGHTY-SEVEN YEARS OLD AND I DON'T HAVE A LIFE! THERE'S NOTHING IN IT FOR ME!"

I give her the check and I leave.

I begin to go around to laboratories, and there's no laboratory that will test for this stuff. They look at it and they say, "We don't test human beings for these things." I finally find one in Monroe, New York— maybe they were in cahoots with Dr. Axe—that will do it for a thousand dollars. Uninsured. But I go through with it. I pay the bill and they draw more blood from me than I've ever had drawn before, and then they give me a big cardboard carton for the twenty-four-hour urine collection. It's like a milk carton with a handle; I have to carry it everywhere for twenty-four hours and collect all my urine. I'm ducking behind trees in Central Park; I'm in therapy with it; I'm in the theater with it between my legs; I'm riding on the subway with it between my legs. And I made the mistake of eating asparagus the day before, and people are moving away from me like I'm a Bowery bum. It's awful.

I get it all down; I get the results. The laboratory sends the results in to Dr. Axe, and then he calls me, or his mother does, for a consultation. I come in, and he gets out all my papers and studies them and looks across at me and says, "Well, now we know the culprit. Vanadium. Your vanadium is off the chart."

I say, "Vanadium. I never heard of it. What is it?"

"A rare element used to toughen steel. To make it more shock-resistant. In other words, you are filled with rare heavy metal. Vanadium."

I said, "Well, it's great to be rare, but I really don't know where it could come from. None of my friends have it. Where would I get vanadium?"

"Sea cucumbers and sea anemones."

"I've never eaten them!"

"No. But big fish eat them, and I'll bet you just love big fish, don't you. I bet you just love them."

"Yeah, I eat that every day."

"You've got to give them up. You know that? That's where the vanadium comes from, it comes from your big fin fish, your tuna. You can't have any more salmon. You can't have any more tuna. You can't have any more swordfish. You have to give them up. I'd also give up all crustaceans, all shellfish, all lobsters. And chicken and turkey."

I said, "Give up big fish? I can't imagine life without big fish. But why the chicken and turkey?"

"They get fed fish, see? They feed chicken and turkey ground fish, that's what it is. You see, it's all in the food chain. I think you'd better give up everything. I think you'd better give up all canned goods, give up all tobacco, give up drinking alcohol, any marijuana, any coffee, please, give up caffeine, all that, and just eat raw vegetables. Just eat raw vegetables. Eat them raw. Just eat raw vegetables. I mean, no one ever cooked vegetables in the old days. They only cooked them because people had wooden false teeth. There's no reason to cook vegetables. Raw. Everything raw. Please. Begin today."

What a shock. It's terrifying. This man has frightened me into doing this. I start on a raw vegetable diet, and I am overwhelmed by it. I go into the Grand Union supermarket to shop. What am I looking at? It's like an abstraction. I walk up and down the aisles through a football field full of food that isn't food. I used to think of a supermarket as a place to go buy food. I would just fill the shopping cart—I never had a list, I'd just take my shopping cart and go up and down the aisles, choosing what I liked, whatever I liked, whatever I saw, whatever I saw out of my good eye. I took things I liked! I ate things I liked!

I walk in there now—nothing was available to me under this new regime. It was a wasteland, except for that little corner where there are vegetables you can eat raw. And they've got these automatic sprayers going on, to make the vegetables look good. But they're not good, because everything gets soggy under the sprayer. The celery is soggy when you get it out. I was bored with it! I was so bored that I started looking for exotic vegetables. I would go to the farmer's market in New York City at Union Square. Every Wednesday and Saturday the Pennsylvania Dutch people bring in fresh produce and stuff. I'm looking for all sorts of exotic turnips, something different in the vegetable department. I'm there one Saturday, and I notice something wonderful. A woman is selling farm-raised trout. I think, How great! They're raised in the Catskills. At last, a fish I can eat! There's no way these trout are running into sea cucumbers up there in the Catskills!

So I go up to her; I'm buying four of them, and I'm so excited, I'm chatting with her. As she's wrapping the trout in a newspaper, I ask, "By the way, what do you feed your trout?"

She says, "Chicken."

Also, I've given up drinking alcohol, which is an enormous event for me, because, certainly, after my mother's death the only religious ritual that survived in our home was cocktail hour. And I always celebrated it. If I wasn't working at night, I would celebrate it. If I was working, I'd celebrate it after I worked. But you know, what do you do if you don't drink? If you don't drink, your day is just one big "AAAAAAAAAAA AAAAAAAAAAAAAAAAAAAAAAAAAAAAA AAAAAAAAAAAAAAAAAAAAAAAAAAAAA AAAAAAAAAAAAAAAAAAAAAAAAAAAA AAAAAAAAAAAAAAAAAAAAAAAAAAAAA AAAAAAAAAAAAAAAAAAAAAAAAAAAAA AAAAAAAAAA—BED! It's a bore; there's no relief; there's no gestalt. There's no shift of gears. There's no change of consciousness. There's no relaxation. There's just too much reality.

But I'm being a good boy. I've given it everything, and I'm eating raw vegetables, and I'm also going to Dr. Axe's Food Combining lectures. Dr. Axe has small group lectures so people can save money by not having to pay for a private consultation. What he does is talk about how you should work with food combinations to make your eyes better. There are about four or five of us huddled around his desk. I'm the only one with a macula pucker. No one else has a macula pucker. A variety of people have macula degeneration, but that's not the same. They have detached retinas, a little glaucoma, a little cataract. That kind of condition.

We're gathered around his desk, all bunched together, and his brother Don has got the earphones on. He's tape-recording so they can sell you the tapes after the lecture.

Dr. Axe starts out with, "All right, people. Let's start with *A,* for amino acids. Now, amino acids are the building blocks of what?"

A woman shouts out, "Protein!"

"Very good, but please. Raise your hand, please. Now I don't want to be a policeman, but I want people to raise their hands here." He's treating us like a seventh-grade biology class. "Now, remember, the stomach does not digest these proteins. It turns them into amino acids. The stomach does not digest protein. What does it digest?"

The same woman cries out, "Amino acids!"

"Amino acids, very good," says Dr. Axe. "Now, would you eat fruit before or after a meal?"

And again this same woman pipes up like a class know-it-all and says "After! I always eat my fruit after a meal."

Dr. Axe says, "Wrong. Now just say you ate a steak.

51

Say you ate a steak by mistake. Just say you ate one. And then you ate a banana afterwards. The steak would digest much slower than the banana, and the banana would just sit on top of it, and it would begin to rot and putrefy, and it would cause explosive bowel movements, and I'll bet you have them, don't you? I'll bet you have them!"

In the middle of all this craziness, the eighty-seven-year-old mother comes in with some tearsheet that she says I'd filled out months ago, and she screeches, "MR. GRAY IS GUILTY!"

"Stop, Mother, please—"

"MR. GRAY IS GUILTY!"

"Mother, please, we're tape-recording."

"MR. GRAY IS GUILTY! HE COOKS HIS CORN. IT SAYS HERE HE COOKS HIS SWEET POTATOES. HE COOKS HIS BEETS. HE COOKS HIS TURNIPS. HE EVEN COOKS HIS EGGPLANT! DOESN'T HE UNDERSTAND HE'S GOT TO EAT IT ALL RAW? RAW! RAAAAAAAAW!"

I just get out of there. I don't go back to the Food Combining lectures, but I have to tell you that I do continue with the raw vegetable program. I'm determined to do it. I'm so frightened about my other eye. It's almost breaking Renée and me up because of the intestinal gas it's causing. It's horrible.

I'm not having any sugar. No alcohol. I'm not smoking any cigarettes or drinking any caffeine. I've given up everything. Sex, too. I didn't realize that all of these things were interconnected in a funny way. The raw vegetables did not make me feel sexy.

I'd entered what Renée's mother calls the Bermuda Triangle of Health, which is pretty terrifying. She says that between fifty years old and fifty-three is the Bermuda Triangle of Health. Things start going wrong with you then, but if you make it through, then you live to be a ripe old age. My God, she had a heart attack at fifty-one; and her husband, Renée's father, died at fifty-two of cancer; Renée's mother's brother had a stroke at fifty; my mother killed herself at fifty-two. The Bermuda Triangle of Health.

I was coming into it, and I was feeling lonely, because I was the only one I knew with a macula pucker. My eye doctor said many people have them, they come in to see him, but he won't give me any names or any telephone numbers, because he's a professional. He won't share those patients with me.

So I put an ad in the *Village Voice*. I put it on the back-page bulletin board. It says, "Macula Pucker Club. Does anyone else have one? Let's share stories."

All I got was a letter from some retina specialist who wanted to scrape me.

Around this time, I'm called in by my eye doctor for an examination, because he wants to see if my condition is deteriorating. I'm sitting there, alone in the waiting room, no longer bringing a book to read, just munching on a raw sweet potato. I go through the ritual of getting my pupils dilated. Just after the nurse puts the drops in, this man comes out of the office with this drooping eye. It's really terrifying. He looks like a bloodhound. I say, "Nurse, what was that?"

She says, "Oh, that's the drooping eye. That's the drooping eye."

I say, "Where does it come from?"

She says, "Oh, that's one of the results sometimes from the macula pucker operation."

"You're kidding."

"Oh, but it's correctable, you know. Then you have to have corrective plastic surgery."

I said, "My God, they didn't tell me about the drooping eye!" I was more freaked out than ever. I didn't want to go into a hospital. This puts me into a bubble fantasy. I didn't want medicine. I wanted magic, and that's all I was thinking about as I was sitting there. I mean, I wanted Jesus to walk into that waiting room the way he used to in the old days with the multitudes and *Bing!* the blind shall see and *Bing!* the deaf shall hear and *Bing!* the lame shall walk. I wanted E.T. If only E.T. would come in and take his little hot magic finger and touch me right on my pucker.

That's what I'm thinking about as I'm sitting there; I'm fantasizing about magic. I believe in magic. I believe that there has to be real magic if there are tricks in the world, because what is a trick, if not an imitation of real magic? I hadn't had a lot of real experiences with magic. But I had one. One that stayed with me. One was enough. It was a very, very strong experience for me.

I was traveling in Australia with my monologue in 1986, and I was going on to Bali. When I got to Bali, I was pretty freaked out because I have this other disease besides the eye problem. The disease is, when I am traveling and I get to a new place, I start regretting all the things I didn't do in the place I just left. And so I think that I have to go back and do them. And that's all I can see. All I can see is this internal film of the place I've just left.

When I got to Bali, I was in beautiful Bali picturing myself scuba diving with my friends in the Great Barrier Reef in Australia, which I hadn't done, and which I could have been doing had I not gone to Bali. I was really torn and I was walking down the main street of Ubud muttering to myself, and someone recognized me from a show of mine he'd seen in Boston, and he said, "You look in really bad shape. Why don't you let me take you to see this healer who is a really great guy."

So he takes me outside Ubud to this small area that is the healer's family compound. He's right in the middle, and the whole family's living around him, watching him heal or perform white magic. He's in a kind of three-sided bamboo hut with a thatched roof. He was doing these amazing exorcisms. People would come in possessed by devils. Three men were holding down this woman; he just said, "Have a seat," like a dentist would.

He has a jolly, wonderful smile and I like him immediately because he's laughing all the time, at me, at everything. He's got a mouth full of gold teeth; he doesn't speak much English, but he throws his head back and laughs at almost everything I say for some reason. I don't know why. I come to him and confess that I've come because I have this disease that won't let me be in Bali, because although he sees me there in front of him, I'm not there in my mind. And I want to get there. Wholly there. He laughs at this and says he's never heard of such a disease. He wants to send me to a hospital for a shot. He says maybe they could take care of it there.

But before he dismisses me, he shows me these magical drawings that he has all rolled up, like scrolls, and he says, "Go through these and see if there's one that you can relate to."

I go through them; they're little eight-by-ten drawings of Balinese icons that his grandfather had done with pen and ink on rice paper. I find one drawing that I immediately identify with.

It's of a little man with four legs and a grass skirt, bare chest, no head. I like this very much. He has no head, but he's still having a good time.

You can just tell by his eyes; they're in his chest. His eyes are twinkling in his chest and his nose is in the center of his body. He had no mouth, which I could relate to. I say, "This I think I can work with. What do we have to do?"

He tells me that I have to give him some Balinese money for it, and he does a ceremony. He invests the little man with power, and he chants, he sings a prayer, he lights incense and adds some flowers, then blows through a coconut. Then he says, "Take the man now. Hang him over your bed. Light incense for him, bring him flowers, talk to him, and you'll soon be in Bali."

So I do. I put the little man over the bed; I bring him flowers. I don't talk a lot to him. I'm a little embarrassed to talk aloud to him; I feel very self-conscious. It's like one of those relationships: flowers, but not a lot of talking.

I bring the little man back to the United States, frame him, and bring him up with me to the MacDowell Colony in the New Hampshire woods, where I was going to write my book, *Impossible Vacation*. I thought, I know it's going to be a lonely process; why not have him there as a companion? So I bring him into my cabin and I put him on the mantelpiece. When I come in to write in the morning, I say, "Hi, little man! I'm just going to make a little coffee and roll a cigarette, and then I'm going to start writing. And then, maybe when I finish writing, we'll go for a walk together, and you'll see the New Hampshire woods. They're really different from Bali. It's springtime now in New Hampshire, and it's not really very green, but the buds are out and it has a kind of austere beauty. It gets greener later in the season but it's never as green as Bali." I'd say things like that to him.

But every day I'd get so involved in my writing that I'd forget about taking him out for a walk.

Then, one day I'm charging for the door to go out for my walk, and I hear this lonely little voice say, "What about the walk? What about the walk?"

I turn and I go to the mantel and I put him in my arms, cradling him the way you might a baby, and I go outside, aiming his eyes up at the clear blue sky. It's early spring. There, about seventy-five feet from the cabin, is a huge maple tree with red buds on it. It's about fifty feet tall. The whole top part of the tree is hopping, teeming with sparrows. As I'm aiming the little man's eyes up at it, the thought occurs to me that if I call a sparrow, it will come and land on me.

Now, I don't even call it. All I do is have the thought come to me, and a sparrow swoops down and begins to circle my head, so close in that I can feel the wings in my ears. I can hear them fluttering in my ears. I have chills. I am very high at this moment, and I feel very, very superb. This birds lands on my left shoulder and simply sits there, breathing. I'm breathing with it. I feel just like St. Francis, just standing there breathing with the bird. I feel very blessed.

I freeze, trembling, with the little man in my arms, and after a few moments the bird takes off . . . and it's gone.

So I knew there was magic in the world.

As I'm sitting there, remembering that moment, a

woman comes and sits down next to me and breaks my reverie in the waiting room. She turns to me and she says, "Hello."

And I turn, and I say, "Oh, hi."

We begin talking, and it turns out that this woman next to me has a macula pucker. And we hug!

It was absolutely incredible.

"I can't believe it, you're the first person—"

"Oh, you're kidding—"

"No, no. Let's compare notes—"

Back and forth, back and forth. I said to her, "What are you going to do about yours?"

"Well, I don't know. I have to make up my mind about the operation by Tuesday."

"By Tuesday! Oh my God, there but for the grace of God go I. I wouldn't want to have to make up my mind any day. I'm just kind of cruising, if you know what I mean. Do you think you'll do it?"

"Oh, I don't know if I'll do it. You know, I'll tell you, I once worked in a big city emergency room, and if you knew what I knew about hospitals, you wouldn't go near—"

"I know, I know, that's what all my friends say. All my friends say that. But have you tried alternative therapies?"

"Oh, I've tried many alternative therapies. There's only one that I haven't tried—and I may do this because I have a friend in Idaho who had a breast tumor removed by this Filipino psychic surgeon."

A Filipino psychic surgeon? Why didn't I think of that! "You're kidding. What happened?"

"He reached right into her breast. No cutting, no incision, nothing. He just pulled out—"

"Where does she live?"

"Idaho."

"Do you have her number?"

"Yes, I can give you any information you want on her."

"Please, please. I've got to get it. I've got to find out about that. I'd forgotten all about psychic surgeons. I'd seen a film on them some years ago, but I had forgotten all about them."

At this point, the nurse comes out and says, "The doctor will see you now, Mr. Gray."

I said, "Well, I'm not ready to see the doctor. I'm off to the Philippines!"

I call the woman in Idaho, and she gives me all the information. I actually called her—this is totally unlike me. I did it. I flew to the Philippines; I flew to Manila, without drinking once on the plane. I arrive, and I fly off to the north immediately to meet this healer named Pini Lopa, also known as the "Elvis Presley of psychic surgeons."

I find out why when I arrive.

I get there; I check into my hotel, and I go over to his place, which is called the Paramount Inn—it used to be the Red Monkey Disco—and he is there, not operating, as it turns out, because it's evening, but entertaining forty Japanese who are all there to be operated on. Actually, twenty have come for operations, and the other twenty have come to photograph the others while they're being operated on.

They're all there. There's no booze at all. It's a totally vegetarian gathering. There's Pini Lopa, and he's about fifty-seven years old. He's got gold chains around his neck; he's got powder-white hair that's cut in a Little Lord Fauntleroy style. He's in a powder-blue suit, wearing these Palm Beach–white lattice leisure shoes, and he's singing Frank Sinatra songs out of tune, with a band backup. He's got a Desi Arnaz/Ricky Ricardo, babba-loo kind of energy, like a performer from Vegas. He's singing "I did it my way," chain-smoking cigarettes. He sounds like Leonard Cohen without the passion.

He's supposed to be the top psychic surgeon who operated on this woman! I'm saying to myself, No judgment! No judgment! I'm just going to hang in here, take it easy. I made it here without having any drinks on the plane. I'm just going to try to relax and maintain my diet and go through with this thing.

After he takes a little break, and the band takes a break, I introduce myself. He's smoking up a storm, and he's really a cocky little guy, just incredible. I start talking to him.

I tell him that I was sent by this woman; he

remembers the woman. I tell him it is for an eye problem. Oh, he assures me that he's very good at eyes. In fact he's been known to pull an eye right out of the skull, lift it up, display it, wash it off, and put it back into the person's eye socket.

I said, "How do you reconnect the veins after that? How do they get all hitched up?"

He said, "We don't know. This is a mystery."

I can't believe this is going on. I go back to my hotel, and I get very little sleep that night.

The next morning, I'm supposed to go in for the operation. Nine-thirty is when I'm supposed to go in. And I have the choice to be operated on, or to observe the operations. So I have to see what I feel about it.

So I arrive, and first everyone's praying. There's a chapel. The Japanese have a Shinto shrine; I'm in front of Jesus. I don't know what to do with him. I'm mainly just sitting there thinking, What am I doing, what am I doing, what am I doing. After the praying is done, we go down this long corridor to enter the operation chamber. On the walls of the corridor are pictures of Pini Lopa performing operations. It's worse than the Mayo Family Clinic book. There are color photos of him, beginning to pull an eye out of the socket. Pictures of him pulling hemorrhoids out of someone's ass.

And at the end of this long corridor is a big crucifix. Some people are bowing and genuflecting to it. You have to realize that we're in the Philippines, where at

Easter time they actually crucify themselves, nail themselves to crosses.

But what I was about to see—I was completely unprepared for. I couldn't believe my eye. It was like a Halloween situation. Like when a kid is going into a Halloween funhouse? That's what I felt like. I felt like a frightened little kid when I walked into that room.

This operating room is divided in half, between the observation area—there are a lot of Japanese in there with videocameras set up—and the operating arena. There's a railing there, and there are about fifteen or twenty Japanese in just their underwear. The women are bare-breasted. There, under the fluorescent light, is a table with a plastic cover. Pini is standing there, with his eyes rolled up in his head, in a semi-trance, wearing a blue surgical gown, a butcher's apron, and white Palm Beach leisure shoes. A picture of Christ is behind him, and at the end of the table are two men with mops.

I decide I'm going to watch that day.

It begins. Here's what I saw. The Japanese who were there and who were ready to be operated on run up. The first woman lies down on the operating table. Pini puts his hand on her belly and his fingers seem to go right into her stomach. Blood shoots up into the air, six feet into the air, hitting the other naked Japanese. They're all shouting, "Woo! Oooh! Woooow!" like little children running under a bloody sprinkler in summertime. Pini's men are down on the floor with the

63

mops, mopping the blood up. This woman jumps off the table and goes around to the other end of the line, getting ready to go again.

A man jumps up on the table. Pini seems to reach into his stomach and pull out what looks like a meatball the size of a cantaloupe. He hurls it into a plastic bucket. This man gets up and goes around to the other side of the table. A woman gets up on the table, and Pini begins to work on her Adam's apple. What looks like this huge tongue of yellow and green pus comes out of her neck. He's catching it in a cup. She goes around the table and comes around the other side. Each one of them is paying three hundred dollars every time he touches them. And believe me, he's not going anywhere in the room to get stuff. It appears that his hands are empty, and that he is really pulling this stuff out of these people.

Another man gets up on the table, and Pini pulls out big bloody grapes this time and begins to handle them like a kid playing with his own shit. He hurls them down on the man's chest. Pini's wife comes over with gauze to sop them up, and throws them into a bucket. The man goes around again. A Japanese man walks up to the table, lies down on his stomach, pulls his pants down, exposes his firm, round rump, and Pini just starts reaching in and up. "Hold still, hold still, hold still," he says and out comes what looks like spaghetti with red meat sauce. It's supposed to be hemorrhoids. *Thupp!* he hurls them into the bucket. That man goes around; everyone goes through one more time, has the exact same thing done to them, and then Pini says, "Finished!"

Pini crosses himself, he crosses everyone, blesses them, goes over and bows to the crucifix on the wall, blesses himself in front of it, bends over, wipes some blood off his white lattice leisure shoes, lights a cigarette, and leaves.

I go back to my hotel and have my first drink.

I have twelve of them in fact. Twelve San Miguel beers. I'm ripped, and I have no one to talk to. The Japanese aren't speaking any English. I'm thinking, Whoa, my God, what's going to happen to me? How could I spend all my money on coming to a place like this? Was I crazy? What a waste of money. I can't go through with this operation! I can't. "Ohhh, God. Give me another beer." The only people who speak English are the Filipino waiters, and I'm saying, "Oh my God, I went to Pini Lopa today. What a mess!"

One waiter looks at me and says, "Pini Lopa? Oh sir, if you to to Pini Lopa and you believe, you will be healed. But if you do not believe you must go home, because you must believe in order to get healed."

"Is belief a prerequisite? I didn't know that. I thought Pini was going to be like Jesus or E.T. One touch. No blood. God, God, God, help me, give me another drink."

"Sir, please, you must believe. You must believe in Pini Lopa."

"I don't believe in anything. Doubt is my bottom line.

The only thing I don't doubt is my own doubt. And give me another beer."

"But sir, you have a Creator. Who is your Creator? Don't you believe in your Creator?"

"I don't know who my Creator was. I always thought I was idiopathic. You know. No known cause."

"But sir—"

"Oh God, God, what am I going to do? I wish I could get on the telephone. I don't know what time it is in the States. Oh God God God—"

"Sir, you are a very religious man, I can tell."

"Why do you say that?"

"You keep praying. All you say is, 'Oh God, oh God, oh God.' This is praying."

I go to bed, but I can't sleep. All I can see is meatballs flying through the air in my room. It's a nightmare. I finally get a little sleep and I wake up and realize what it is that I'm terrified of; I haven't faced it. It's AIDS! Of course, every American is blood phobic. My good God, the Japanese don't seem to be upset about it.

They say, "Oh, no AIDS in Tokyo, not really, no."

The Filipinos are telling me there's no AIDS in the Philippines either. They tell me that there has been no infection, ever, from psychic surgery. In the entire history of psychic surgery there's never been any known infection. They're like the people at Bondi Beach in Australia, who used to tell me that there hadn't been shark attacks in fifty years.

I said, "It's time. And I'm the one."

I was very paranoid. I knew that I had to speak to Pini before the operation. I ask for a private consultation. I can tell that he's really annoyed with me, the only American there, acting odd, hypochondriacal, frightened.

I ask him, "Please, can you work with me privately in my hotel room?"

"No."

"Please, just this once, look, if you could just wash your hands with alcohol and come over to my room—"

"No. No. We do only the group operation here. What is your problem?"

"I'm afraid of AIDS."

"No, no. Don't worry. I can't operate on people with the AIDS. I'd like to be able to, but—I tried, you see, one time, and the person didn't know he had the AIDS, but my hands they know. They will not enter. They will not penetrate the body. So you have no fear, you see, for that.

"Also, if you are thinking of the AIDS all the time, and I'm sure you do, you will get it. You will manifest it through your thought, you see."

At this point, I tried to tell him the story about the man who was told that if he stirred a pot of water long enough without once thinking of elephants, it would turn into gold. . . .

But Pini didn't want to hear that story. He wanted to operate, and it was time. He left me; I went into the operation chamber, and I thought, I've got to get on that table. The only way I was going to get on that table was if I got right in with the Japanese—just got right in the middle of that kamikaze energy. The way they would jump on that table! It was incredible. I have never seen people move with such determination and lack of doubt. They were all laughing, having such a good time.

I stripped to my red underwear, I got in the middle, and the Japanese began to go up to the table. Out come the bloody grapes again! Out come the meatballs! My time comes, and I jump on. It's like jumping right into a Francis Bacon painting. Right into a Bosch painting. Right into a Catholic morgue. All this stuff is all on the floor, reeking of blood. I'm lying there quaking on the table, crying out, "It's my eye! Remember, my left eye! Please! Don't pull any meatballs out of me!"

Pini is looking down at me like I'm crazy.

First, he wipes his hands off. He's got short sleeves on. He rinses his hands off in what looks like a bucket of blood, really. His hands are a little pink, all right, but clear. He shows me his hands; there is nothing in them. Nothing in either one. His sleeves are rolled up.

He picks up some cotton gauze, and of course that's where the Amazing Randi and all the debunkers say the fakers hide the blood—in the gauze. But it's almost like he could read my mind. He opens the gauze to show me: nothing in that, either. You know: Disbeliever, Doubting Thomas, here you go.

He begins and heads right for my eye with his fingers.

He is pushing in to either side of my eye, and at that moment, I really feel like my eye is a vagina and his two fingers are erect bloody penises coming at me. I'm having a shutdown virgin response here.

As soon as his fingers hit my eye, blood gushes out. Blood clots. Blood. Blood! It's pouring down and someone is sopping it off my face. It doesn't feel like it's coming out of my eye, but it's coming from somewhere! He pulls his fingers out, the blood stops, and I run—not to the end of the line, but to the men's room— immediately, to look at my eye. There's no blood there! There's no leftover blood, and the eye's not any better. But Pini tells me that he wants to do this to me again, and it's going to be fifty dollars each time he touches me. He wants to do it for seven days, twice a day—that's fourteen operations. That's what he wants to do to heal me.

I think, My God, my God! Why can't he be like E.T.? Come on! Fourteen operations! I thought this man had power. I just couldn't do it; I couldn't feel comfortable. I couldn't force myself to be comfortable with this man.

I kept hearing my childhood friends from Barrington, Rhode Island—the ones who asked me what it would take to make me go to a doctor—saying, "What if you went to this guy who started pulling meatballs out of you the size of melons. Would you go to a doctor thennnnn?"

"YES!!!"

I get on the plane to go back to New York. I'm not sure, but I think I might have the operation. I'm just happy to get out of the Philippines. And I was so relieved to be on the plane, because for me, airplanes are the only sacred nondenominational place of prayer left in the world. You know, everyone's praying in their own way during takeoff. I certainly was. I was visualizing the little Balinese man as I took off.

When I get back I'm still not sure. I'm talking with my doctor and he says he would like me to have a pre-op exam. I can always change my mind about the operation, but I should come in for the preoperative, and in a week's time, he can either operate or not operate.

I go in for the pre-op. He says to come in to the office on Friday because he doesn't have a lot of patients then, it'll be empty, and he can see me very quickly.

I go back to that waiting room. They dilate my pupils; I'm sitting there in the waiting room, pretty used to this by now, waiting in the fuzz.

I see this person come out of my doctor's office. In my dilated condition I see this little guy backing out in a pinstripe suit, making real jerky movements, kind of like in a Buster Keaton movie. He's waving like a wind-up toy. Like he's this . . . automatic something, I don't know what.

He turns and starts walking toward me. I'm amazed

and shocked to see that he's got on one of those rubber Nixon masks that we used to buy in joke shops when Nixon was president. What the hell is going on in my doctor's office? He's walking right toward me, and as he gets closer I realize that it *is* Richard Nixon.

Richard Nixon is walking directly toward me—with intent. As though he were going to come up to me and say, "Hi, I saw *Swimming to Cambodia,* and I loved it!"

I think, No, wait a minute, maybe his pupils are dilated too, and he thinks I'm Ralph Lauren.

He walks right up to me, and I say, "Oh. Hi."

He says nothing, and then he walks out.

He just leaves. I go into my doctor's office. My doctor smiles with his Buddha smile and asks, "How was the Philippines, Mr. Gray?"

I say, "Please, don't ask me, don't ask. But let me ask you something. Was that Richard Nixon who just left here?"

"Oh yes. Nothing the matter with *him.*"

"Well, there is no justice in the world, is there?"

"Look, I don't think Nixon did anything worse than Reagan. Really—"

I dropped it. I didn't want to start arguing with my doctor about politics if we were going to go ahead with the operation.

But you know the odd thing? It was seeing Richard Nixon come out of my doctor's office that gave me the faith and the courage to have the operation.

I also couldn't have done it without Renée. I could

not have gone through the operation without her. She held my hand right to the operating room. I was terrified. That great fear day. They gave me a local anesthetic. I could hear most of the conversation while they worked on me. The doctors were chatting away about a party they had been to the night before. Gossiping while they were doing microsurgery. They're cutting the white of my eye in two places. They're putting in a scraper/peeler and a pump, and a magnifying glass, through the iris, and rock 'n' roll is playing through most of it. I remember "Crocodile Rock," Elton John. Afterwards they blew a bubble in my eye—a gas bubble, I didn't know they'd do that—to prevent glaucoma. They put a big patch over my eye, and I had to keep my face down to keep the bubble from breaking—for fourteen days.

The doctor gave me a videotape of the operation to take home. He titled it "Swimming to Macula Pucker." He had a great sense of humor.

I got home, and Renée really nursed me. In order to keep the bubble from breaking—I wasn't even allowed to roll over in my sleep—Renée put pillows on either side of my body in bed. I spent most of my time facedown on the floor.

I had to walk with my head down, eat with my chin to my chest.... We applied for the Books for the Blind Program, so I could go get books on tape at the Library for the Blind, unabridged books. I remember looking at the dog shit and bubble gum on the sidewalk as I walked up to get *The Miracle Worker,* Renée guiding me.

I had to watch the video of the operation through mirrors, because I couldn't look up at the TV set. Oh my God, what a thing! Talk about Pini Lopa's operation —what a miracle of science this video showed. First of all, my eye is magnified. My macula is like a giant sun. Then you see a little pincer, like a crab's claw, of the doctor, pulling this gossamer skin off it, without ever touching the retina, without ever touching the macula. This fine gossamer. You can see right through it. It's like cobwebs floating off a giant sun.

The camera pulls back and you're in Snowland. You're in the South Pole. Renée says, "Oh God, we're in white snow. What is this?" Suddenly, you see magnified stitches the size of rope. They're stitching up the white of my eye. It's like *The Andalusian Dog,* seen through a telescope. Renée runs to the bathroom at this point.

I'm watching this, saying, "This is not my eye! This is just a movie!"

After fourteen days, I go into the hospital to have the patch removed. I know this is supposed to be the dramatic part of the film: *Will the man see again or not?*

It's nothing as dramatic as a movie. They pull off the patch. *Aaaah, auurh.* . . . It's like driving in a rainstorm without windshield wipers. That's what it looks like. It looks like the bottom of an empty Coke bottle. It's not great. Things are less distorted, but they are really blurry. Also, I don't know if it's any better, because I can't remember what it was like before it puckered. I have nothing to compare it to. But mainly I'm happy to have right eye vision. My God, I'm suddenly, Oooh, I realize that my right eye is really important. I'm very protective of it. I'm on the lookout for pinkies when I dance. I'm very cautious.

I begin to realize that there are tricks in the world, and there's magic in the world. But there's also reality. And I have to begin to cope with the fact that I'm a little cockeyed. I feel like I've got a hair that I want to keep brushing out of my eye. But I don't have a whole lot of time to dwell on it. Because Renée—who is over to my right—wants to get married.

And she's very clear as to why, very clear.

She says, "Spald? You know when you were in the hospital, every time I tried to get access to you, they wouldn't let me see you, because I was the girlfriend. Now you're going to get older, and you're going to get sicker a lot more and you'll be in the hospital again. I think it's time we got married."

She's got me on that one. She really has me, so I propose to her in front of a witness—my therapist. I'm very nervous about it.

She's nervous about it, too. She's making all sorts of Freudian slips after I propose. She says things like "Spald, we really do have to set our deading weight."

We set the deading weight for August. It was only October, so there was plenty of time to get to know each other. . . .

We rented a house in Wainscot, out on Long Island, for the month of August, the idea being that we'd be there for a couple of weeks, then have the wedding in mid-August, then have a honeymoon in the house. I got out there and I have to tell you, I got really nuts. I got really—I got frightened. I got nuts. I don't know why. I don't know what it was about. Why was I so afraid to get married? I mean, I was like—a MANIAC!!!!! I was groaning. I was pouting. I was pacing up and down the beach like a frantic man who had lost his contact lenses. What was going on? What was going on? Every time Renée would show me the place on the beach where we were going to get married, I would take this wide sweep around it, looking at it like, *Whooooo!* Look at that place! Wow!

I'd pace up and down the beach, looking more and more at women. I really noticed them, really started checking them out like I'd never done before. I'd say to myself, *Why not her?* You know? In order to diffuse that, I would just cover my right eye and they'd all blur. Men and women would be equal blurs.

The one thing that kept me sane during that time was bodysurfing. I love to bodysurf, particularly when the water's cold; it really grounds me and wakes me up at the same time. I was in the water bodysurfing every day.

One day I was in, after we'd had a big storm that had created a sea puss. I had never been in a sea puss before, wasn't even aware sea pusses existed, until someone told me what they were.

A sea puss is not like an undertow, but it's an odd thing in which the waves come in and break up against each other and back up, so there's a condition where the wave goes up and then goes backwards. And I was riding up on a wave, and then down. I thought I was just bobbing up and down. I didn't know I was being pulled so far out until I saw Renée on shore, and I realized, suddenly, like a little kid, *Whooo!* I'm far out!

Aye yi yi, I went into a panic. Which you must never do. And I know that. But I couldn't get over the crest of the sea puss, and I was choking. The panic set off my adrenaline. That was pretty bad. Because I was exhausted within thirty seconds. I started to swallow seawater.

I thought, I'd better yell for help. I may be drowning. I've never drowned before. I know I procrastinate and deliberate on almost everything, but I'm not going to take a chance with this one. I'm going to do it. I'm going to yell for help.

So I yell, "RENÉE! HELP!"

She's on shore going, "I can't go swimming now. I just ate." She can't hear me, because the wind is blowing off the shore.

Now this puts me in a real panic, knowing that I can't be heard, that I can't get over the top of this thing. Then the helps start to come. They're big helps; they're existential helps from my toes to my nose.

It's "HELLLLLLLLLLLLLP! I'M DROWNING! HELP, I'M GETTING MARRIED! HELP, I'M GROWING OLD! HELP, I'M GOING BALD! HELP, I'M GOING BLIND! HELP, I'M GOING TO DIE! HELP, I'M GOING TO LEAVE THIS EARTH FOREVER ONE DAY! HELLLLLLLLLLLP!"

But this beach has no lifeguard.

Renée finds three guys on shore and screams, "Get out there! Get out there! Get out there! Save him!"

They say, "But, madam, we don't know anything about lifesaving."

She says, "You're the men. Get out there!"

I see these three distraught faces, frightened men, coming toward me. I know they don't know what to do. That frightens me all the more. But one of them has a yellow boogie board. When I see that yellow boogie board, it's like a gift from heaven. I know that I can swim to it and hang on to it and not pull them down. That's what I'm afraid of doing.

I get on the board; I'm choking and spitting up water. They pull me out of the water, up on the beach, and I'm down on the beach choking up water. They're pulling me up like Christ between them, holding me, trying to take my photograph with them; they won't even give me a break. They recognize me. They said they recognized me from the *Swimming to Cambodia* poster, the way my head was bobbing half out of the water! Art imitates life; life imitates art!

The first guy says, "Hey, my name is Phil Hampton.

Let me introduce myself. I'm a chiropractor from Punxsutawney, Pennsylvania. And if you ever do a monologue about this drowning, please mention my name."

Phil Hampton.

The second guy says, "You know, I had a very decadent summer. I was cheating on my girlfriend; we broke up. I did nothing right. I did nothing good for anyone. Except that I was able to save you from drowning, and it's really made me feel good."

And the third guy says, "Boy, you really got balls. I couldn't yell help like that no matter what was happening to me."

I realized: I just had my bachelor party!

Shortly after this almost-drowning—it was just a matter of days, five days afterwards—Hurricane Bob hits Long Island. Devastates it. All the trees are down; there's no electricity; there's no water.

Renée wakes up hysterical; it's just a few days before the wedding. "My God, what are we going to do? Really? What will we do? The relatives will have to shit in the woods. I don't know. . . . How can we get married? I don't know if we can get married!"

I say, "I think you're right. I think you're right. You know, I see this hurricane as a sign."

She says, "Well, I see it as a challenge."

Renée gets out and organizes. She calls for Porto-Sans; there's going to be a cookout where they can do a barbecue. It's all going to work out. We clean up the trees in the yard.

I'm still terrified, though. At the last minute I want to call it off. I call our lawyer, and I say, "Ron, Ron, I've got cold feet. I can't go through with it."

He says, "Spalding. You're an actor. Act like you want to get married. See what it feels like, c'mon. Be a mensch."

Clear blue sky, high, white, fluffy clouds. It was a late afternoon ceremony down at the beach. Everyone gathered in the area; four-wheel-drive vehicles were buzzing us to see what was going on.

Renée was running toward the whole group, barefoot in her powder-pink Grace Kelly wedding dress. I brought down the little Balinese man to be a witness.

Ron was marrying us. He had joined the Universal Church of God in Fresno, California, for thirty-five dollars. We had written the ceremony together, and he spoke it beautifully, ending with, "May this couple be together for as long as they both shall love."

We run down to the sea together to look out, and then we went back to the house to celebrate.

I drank vodka and I drank white wine and I ate big fish.

I ate steamed vegetables and I ate wedding cake. I drank coffee and I smoked a cigar.

I drank brandy.

And I ate and I drank and I smoked ... *everything* that could make me blind.

Thank you for coming.